Storm Run

The Story of the First Woman
to Win the Iditarod Sled Dog Race

Libby Riddles   *Illustrated by* Shannon Cartwright

*To Mrs Witt-Albeck &
her students!
MUSH ON!
[signature]
July 2004*

PAWS IV

PUBLISHED BY SASQUATCH BOOKS

The arctic blizzard ripped across the tundra. Native Alaskans probably have a word for such a storm. Something that means "wind-driven snow that cuts and freezes bare skin." It was a cold that could kill.

A raven riding the wind dipped toward a spot of color on the ice below. A young woman struggled with the frozen zipper on her sled bag, trying to escape the brutal wind. It hammered her, howling savagely down from the north like a wounded animal. Sky and sea ice dissolved into a world of churning snow. Her huskies were already buried comfortably beneath the drift. Human beings really had no business out in such weather.

She knew she might freeze to death tonight. But she also knew that she might go on to become the first woman to win the Iditarod Sled Dog Race. Right now she was too tired and cold to care which.

Pogo, the family's springer spaniel, was my shadow as I explored the neighborhood woods.

$\mathcal{J}$ grew up in the Midwest and in the Pacific Northwest. As a child, I spent endless days reading books about animals. The woods surrounding our house were always magical, with treasures of hidden flowers, strange mushrooms, and rotting wood that seemed to glow in the dark. There were berries to eat, creeks to wade, and trees to climb. Winters were full of skiing, fast and fun, with the glorious smell of the mountain air.

By the age of five, I was already enjoying a life filled with animals. My parents always had dogs and cats, and tanks of tropical fish, and canaries that the cats would make mincemeat of. When I was six, I got bucked off my neighbor's horse—and got right back on again. I was fascinated with animals and had a way of bringing home any kind of critter who wandered into my path. For a while I dreamed of being a rancher out West, just so I could have as many animals as I wanted.

It was this little girl's dream about living a life surrounded by animals that eventually led me north to Alaska—and to the Iditarod Trail.

In family photos, I was usually the one with the pet. Here I am with my brothers and sisters—and Pogo.

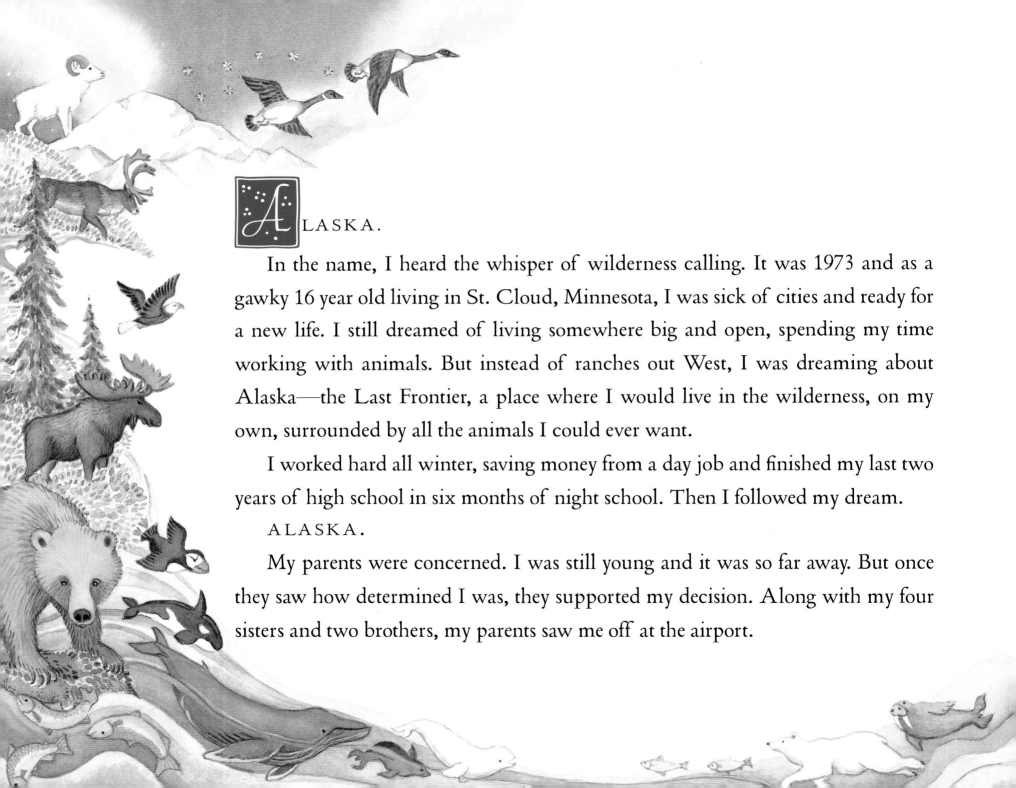

ALASKA.

In the name, I heard the whisper of wilderness calling. It was 1973 and as a gawky 16 year old living in St. Cloud, Minnesota, I was sick of cities and ready for a new life. I still dreamed of living somewhere big and open, spending my time working with animals. But instead of ranches out West, I was dreaming about Alaska—the Last Frontier, a place where I would live in the wilderness, on my own, surrounded by all the animals I could ever want.

I worked hard all winter, saving money from a day job and finished my last two years of high school in six months of night school. Then I followed my dream.

ALASKA.

My parents were concerned. I was still young and it was so far away. But once they saw how determined I was, they supported my decision. Along with my four sisters and two brothers, my parents saw me off at the airport.

I was totally green when I showed up in Alaska, wearing an old, secondhand beaver coat and high-heeled sheepskin boots. I had no idea how to fend for myself, but friends from Minnesota who had moved there earlier helped get me started. It was scary, but exciting too. I just had faith that things would turn out. I settled near Nelchina, in the mountains northeast of Anchorage, and learned to live what Alaskans call "bush-style": building my own cabin, burning wood for heat, carrying water from a mountain stream, and eating moose meat.

Chopping firewood kept me warm in two ways: cutting it and burning it!

I spent three winters in this cabin at Nelchina, training for my first Iditarod races.

One winter day during a grocery run to Anchorage, I ended up in the crowd watching the 1973 Open World Championship Sled Dog Race. *Ssswish!* Teams of huskies flew around corners and then disappeared into the distance, all legs and quiet speed, scattering the sparkling snow. In that moment, I fell in love. Dog mushing was the most exciting and beautiful thing I'd ever seen. The part of me that always felt close to nature began to sing.

A team leaving the starting line of the Open World Championship, the first sled dog race I saw. It is a sprint race, which is much shorter and faster than the Iditarod.

I started building my own sled-dog team. Husky rejects soon surrounded my cabin. If someone had tried to sell me a three-legged dog, I probably would have bought it.

My huskies were a motley gang. Not one was a leader. When I tried to run them, they fought and chewed the sled lines. After breaking up the fights, I would sit on the sled and cry. I wondered if I would ever be a musher. It sure wasn't as easy as it looked. But I kept at it. I made the dogs haul firewood and water for me, and finally they started to behave.

In Teller, we hauled firewood from a beach six miles away to heat our house. That's Minnow and Tip closest to the sled.

In my cabin at night, I would pull my chair close to the stove, turn the kerosene lamp up high, and read about polar explorers. I shivered as I read of Ernest Shackleton and Richard Byrd, trudging for thousands of miles across Antarctic ice, driven to be the first to reach the South Pole. Then I'd blow out the lamp and snuggle down into my cozy sleeping bag, extra glad for the warmth.

Rick McConnell, an Iditarod musher, startled me one day by telling me I should run a race. I thought anyone who ran the long distance sled-dog races was crazy. I was happy just to have the dogs for company and to help me haul the wood and water. But he had a short, five-mile sprint race in mind. What was there to lose? I hooked up my best dogs and astounded myself by winning the race! "Gee, racing might not be so bad after all!" I thought.

The next thing I knew, I was planning to run the Iditarod.

The first place trophy I won in my first race.

My first race was a sprint race. We use a smaller sled and carry no supplies, and we go faster than in a long-distance race like the Iditarod.

I wanted to run the Iditarod Sled Dog Race because it is the ultimate challenge with sled dogs—running across a thousand miles of the roughest country in Alaska. Iditarod mushers are some of the toughest Northerners around. The trail goes over the Alaska Range, up the Yukon River, and over to the Bering Sea, finishing in the historic gold rush town of Nome. I knew it would take me all winter or longer to train for the race, and almost two weeks to run it.

A Sledload of Iditarod Gear

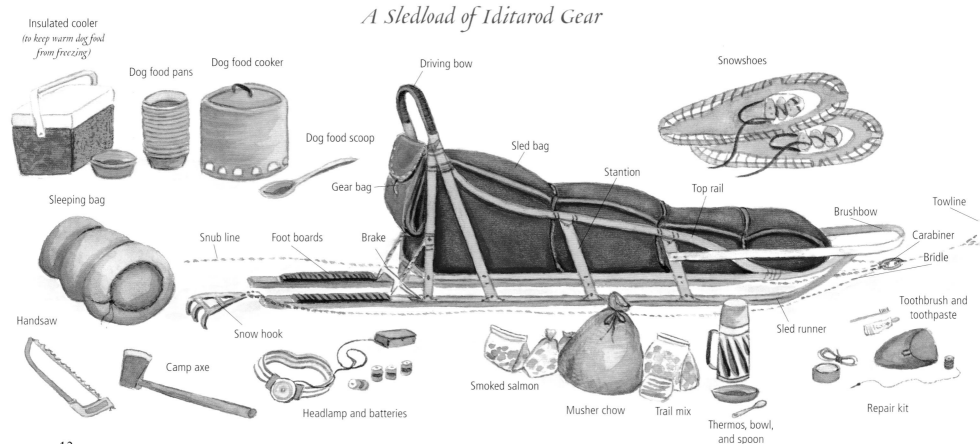

Insulated cooler
(to keep warm dog food from freezing)

Dog food pans

Dog food cooker

Driving bow

Snowshoes

Dog food scoop

Sled bag

Stantion

Top rail

Gear bag

Towline

Sleeping bag

Brushbow

Carabiner

Snub line   Foot boards   Brake

Bridle

Handsaw

Toothbrush and toothpaste

Snow hook

Sled runner

Camp axe

Smoked salmon

Repair kit

Headlamp and batteries

Musher chow   Trail mix

Thermos, bowl, and spoon

There was so much to do! I talked to other mushers and read whatever I could about training and caring for dogs. My friends helped out when they could.

My plan was to spend the winter of 1979 training as though I was going to run the Iditarod that year, but to wait until the next winter to do it. I didn't kid myself about how much experience I needed to finish a thousand-mile marathon.

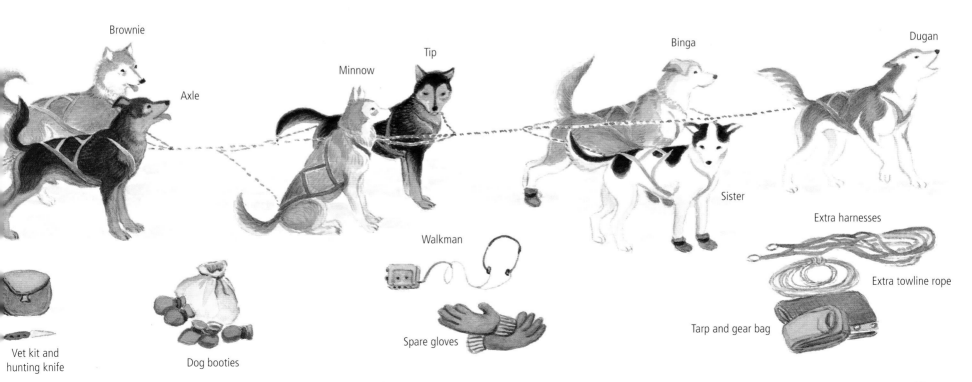

Brownie

Axle

Minnow

Tip

Binga

Dugan

Sister

Extra harnesses

Extra towline rope

Walkman

Tarp and gear bag

Spare gloves

Vet kit and
hunting knife

Dog booties

I worked hard. Living bush-style had taught me the meaning of endurance. It didn't matter if the weather was bad or how I was feeling—I had chores to do and the dogs needed care no matter what. Every day I lugged steaming buckets of food and water to the dogs and shoveled the yard. I bucked up deadwood with a chainsaw and the dogs and I hauled it down the hill on a sled. I melted snow for the dogs in buckets balanced around the stove, and together we hauled "people water" three miles from Nelchina Lodge in five-gallon cans. I

Coming home after a long training run near Nelchina. That's Solo in front, my first leader.

sewed dog booties and nylon collars, and took the dogs on long training runs. It seemed like I was always hungry. Often I'd return home so starved from the long miles on the trail that I'd snack the dogs quickly, and then run to the cabin for a bit of food so I'd have the juice to unharness the team.

I signed up to run the 180-mile Cantwell-Denali Highway Race, to get a taste of what was ahead. Afterward I went over all the mistakes I'd made. I'd taken way too much stuff in my sled. Also, by the time I started the race, I was so tired that later in the race I felt out of it. But I also learned a lot about my dogs. Solo, a spooky, no sense of humor leader I had bought from Iditarod champion Rick Swenson, was the biggest surprise. Before the race, he was still getting used to me, and he wasn't very cooperative. So I tried using two other dogs as leader. But as soon as we hit the race trail, Solo was Mr. Business and led almost the whole way.

I ran my first Iditarod in 1980, when trail conditions were bad. As a rookie, I was too dumb to know things were worse than normal, so I just kept plugging away. And I came in eighteenth out of sixty teams—the second rookie to finish!

Camping out during my first distance race, the Cantwell 180.

Running the Iditarod had been very hard, and I had been cold and tired most of the time. Still, there was something special about the way the race challenged me to be and do my very best. I liked that. And I loved spending all that time with my dogs.

I flew to Teller in a small plane, with thirteen dogs!

Dugan, Bugs, Binga, Axle, and their other brothers were born in a fish camp near Teller. They all grew up to be lead dogs, and four of them became Iditarod stars.

My education continued. I raced in the Iditarod again the next year, full of awe at how extreme conditions could be up on the Arctic coast and amazed at the Native people who somehow thrived there. In the villages we raced through, dog teams were a part of life. In fact, the best dogs came from those villages. Some of the best mushers, too. I decided to move up to there, to the real Alaska, so I could raise and run my dogs in a place where they were still a way of life. So I headed north with a planeload of dogs and sent for Danger, my cat, after I got settled in.

I ended up in the small coastal Native village of Teller, north of Nome, and started working with Iditarod musher Joe Garnie. Joe had grown up in Teller, and I'd met him on the Iditarod Trail. One of my dogs had pups a few weeks after we got to Teller, and I hoped they would grow up to be my new Iditarod stars.

All year long, Joe and I fished for food for the dogs and ourselves. During the short summers, cut salmon glistened richly as it dried on the fish-camp racks. In the fall, wearing our warmest clothes, we fished at night, pulling hundreds of pounds of sparkling, sweet-smelling herring to shore in our beach seine net. Even in the winter we fished, with nets strung through holes in the ice, pulling out northern pike and fat whitefish, which the dogs then hauled back to camp. Sometimes I'd get pretty sore from all the hard work, but I didn't let it stop me.

For hundreds of years, split and dried salmon has been one of the main foods for sled dogs.

The pups grew up following the big dogs on training runs. One slender brown pup was always ahead of the team, leading the way. Every once in a while, he would stop and wait impatiently for the rest to catch up. His name was Dugan.

Dugan's brother, Axle, had a different personality. He was like a babysitter to a litter of pups that belonged to Joe's lead dog, Sister. Sister wanted to get back in the team and wasn't interested in taking care of pups. So Axle stayed behind, huddled under the porch, licking and caring for Sister's litter.

Joe's leader, Sister, eight years old, was the most experienced dog on the team.

In the dog yard in Teller, with Stewpot, one year before I ran the Iditarod.

Axle and Bugs share the couch with Danger, my cat.

The people of Teller helped raise money for me to get into the Iditrod.

By 1985, the year I planned to run the Iditarod, the young dogs were four years old and had grown into tough, lanky huskies. They'd been tested on the Kusko 300 Race and Joe had raced with a combination of our young dogs to a third place finish in the 1984 Iditarod. Not too shabby for their first time out.

People in Teller saw me out in the dog yard every day taking care of my team. They watched from warm, cozy houses as I harnessed up, determined to train in the bitter weather. When no one else would help sponsor an unknown musher like me, the people of Teller pitched in with their bingo money.

Finally, the morning of March 2, 1985 arrived. The teams stretched out at the Iditarod starting line on Fourth Avenue in downtown Anchorage. I gripped the driving bow of my dog sled as the announcer counted down the time. It was hard not to be nervous. The dogs were barking and going berserk with excitement.

Excitement is high as we blast off the starting line in Anchorage, with Joe on the tag sled behind me.

Four brothers made up the heart of my team: shy, furry Binga; Bug-man, who had broken a toe as a pup but was now a great leader; Axle, the well-mannered one; and Dugan, the superstar leader. Minnow and Tip, the twin grandchildren of my first Iditarod leader, Solo, were there, along with lively young Inca, barking and yipping to go.

The oldest dog on the team was Joe's shaggy but savvy leader, Sister. She was mean and she was ugly, but there wasn't one ounce of quit in her. Sister's pups, Stripe and Whitey, ran in the middle. Fat, red Dusty was another of Joe's leaders, but Dusty didn't like to lead for me. Socks, Brownie, Stewpot, and sweet Penny rounded out the rest of my 15-dog team.

"Three, two, one!" the race announcer shouted, and we were off!

Traveling through the streets of Anchorage
with a fresh team was so dangerous that we were allowed
to bring another person along, to help control the sled. So Joe
was riding in a tag sled tied close behind me when we had our first
disaster. The dogs took a short-cut through the woods, bouncing the sled off
trees and crashing through alders.

"Hang on!" I yelled as we went airborne over an old, half-buried
washing machine. The pull of the dogs kept
me upright, but Joe crashed in a heap,

20

crunching his arm. He caught back up to me, bruised and sore, and off we went again. I spent most of that afternoon jamming my brake as we careened around boulders and through metal culverts. When we reached Knik, I dropped Joe off and headed into the Alaska bush on my own.

Running under the stars later that night, exhausted from the long day of racing, I thought about how my bad luck was never as bad as it seemed. First, the brake on my sled had snapped after using it all day—but I'd managed to find a replacement before leaving civilization. Then, later in the afternoon, I practically lost my whole team when I stopped to give them a snack. I had tied them to a tree, but they weren't ready to rest. They snapped the tree like a twig and ran off without me!

The first rule of dog mushing is *never let go of your sled!* If you do, the only thing that will stop the dogs is if the sled or the snow hook accidentally gets caught on something. I grabbed wildly for the snub line, dragging face down in the snow for as long as I could before my hands gave out. For a moment I lay there, not believing how bad my luck was. My team was disappearing down the trail, with my hopes for the race going right along with them. Then I bolted after them, screaming and hollering for them to stop, just in case they'd listen.

My good luck came in the form of two other mushers. Chuck Schaeffer caught up from behind and offered me a lift. A second musher, Terry Adkins, managed to stop and tie up my wayward dog team farther up the trail. None of the dogs was hurt, and I was grateful that the Iditarod was the kind of race where mushers would help each other out.

The snow was really deep in 1985, which meant moose were a problem. The gigantic animals would rather walk on the packed race trail than flounder in deep snow, and the hard-to-reach buds they munched on and the tough traveling made the moose cranky.

Several mushers had run-ins with the moose, including Susan Butcher, a top woman musher. A moose killed two of her dogs before another racer shot the moose. My team came up on one moose, but lucky for me, another musher, Lavon Barve, had already snowshoed a trail around the stubborn animal. I wisely took the detour.

s the miles fell away the pressure began to build. Joe had done well with this same team the year before. Would I be able to do as well? "Don't worry about it," I told myself. "Just do the best you can."

As the teams drew closer to the mountains of the Alaska Range, the weather got worse. At Rainy Pass, we got the bad news. The pass was closed. The pilots hadn't been able to get dog food to the checkpoints beyond. On Day 3, the race was "frozen" for 70 hours. We had to stay put until the pilots could make it through. People from Anchorage donated dog food to be shipped out for our teams. I stretched out the food I had as long as I could. Every couple of hours, I'd melt snow in the cooker and add a little meat to make broth. I found spruce branches and made little beds for the dogs to sleep on.

On the way to Rainy Pass, with Penny and Stewpot "in wheel" (closest to the sled).

At Rainy Pass Lodge, I found an empty bunk. The only problem was one of the other mushers snored so loudly I couldn't sleep. The noise was making me crazy, so I reached down to where I'd seen some pillows, planning to throw one at the snorer. But instead of a pillow, my hand latched on to the face of another sleeping musher! I wasn't sure which one of us was more scared. Someone finally shook the snoring guy, and he quieted down before the whole cabin collapsed.

Huskies have fur like a wolf's, with two layers to keep them warm.

When the weather lifted, teams were allowed to cross over Rainy Pass, in the Alaska Range.

On the morning of Day 6, the race began again. The teams made it across Rainy Pass and over Farewell Burn to Alaska's Interior. Things were going okay until the weather once again shut the race down at the Ophir checkpoint. It was a day and a half before we could leave.

On Day 11 we reached the Yukon, the biggest river in Alaska. The weather got colder and colder as the wind raged from bank to bank, erasing any trail. In the last faint wash of a fading red sunset, I saw a fire winking in the darkness ahead. Two mushers were thawing out, and since it was time for a break anyway, I stopped to snack the huskies and try to get warm.

It was hard to pry myself away from the comforting fire, but I was soon back on the trail, with a chilly night stretching ahead. Before long, we came to a lodge with several sleds pulled up in front. The lights and the smell of food tugged at me, but I had just rested the dogs. It sure was tempting to stop, though. While I was trying to decide, the dogs were trying to pull me up to the lodge. I didn't want them to get bad habits after I'd worked so hard to train them, so up the Yukon we went.

We moved into the blackest of nights. I couldn't make out any runner tracks. In fact, I could barely see the trail. I was either lost—or in first place.

It was 40 degrees below zero when I finally reached the checkpoint at Eagle Island. There, I found out I was in the lead!

Traveling along the edge of the Yukon River at 20 degrees below zero. The temperature would drop another 20 degrees that night.

The next night, on the way to Kaltag, the bottom dropped out. With the sun sinking like a cold gold ball, the temperature plummeted. Around here they call that kind of weather "severe clear."

It was 60 below, so cold I had to pull out my sleeping bag and wear it around me like a cape, just to stay even a little warm. I ran or pedaled constantly to keep my feet from freezing in the damp shoepacs. During that spooky, dangerous night, I cursed the cold like it was some primitive, mad animal. The dogs pulled steadily, the frost of their breath making them look like ghost dogs. The weather didn't seem to bother them at all.

Dugan had been running lead almost all the way. I tried other dogs up front with him, and was surprised that Axle, who had never led before, seemed to do the best.

It seemed to me that he did it because he had a great big heart, and wanted to help however he could. As the northern lights flickered coldly overhead, I thought of how proud I was of these dogs that I'd raised from pups, and how much I loved them all. They didn't know about winning. They just knew they had a job to do and they did it eagerly.

Axle, Dugan's brother, rose to the occasion when I needed another leader.

ARCTIC CIRCLE

SEWARD PENINSULA

KOYUKUK RIVER

YUKON RIVER

Teller

FINISH
Nome
Safety
TOPKOK HILLS
White Mountain
Golovin
Elim
Koyuk
Shaktoolik

Koyukuk
Nulato
Galena
Ruby
Fairbanks

Kaltag

NORTON SOUND

BERING SEA

Salatna

Unalakleet

NORTHERN ROUTE

Cripple

YUKON RIVER

Eagle Island

Ophir
McGrath
Nikolai
Takotna

MT. McKINLEY

Cantwell

Grayling

Anvik

SOUTHERN (1985) ROUTE

Shageluk

FAREWELL BURN

Farewell

Rohn

ALASKA RANGE

Talkeetna

TAKOTNA R.

Iditarod

SUSITNA RIVER

YUKON RIVER

KUSKOKWIN RIVER

KUSKOKWIN MOUNTAINS

Rainy Pass
Finger Lake
Skwentna

Nelchina →

Wasilla
Knik
Eagle River

Bethel

START
Anchorage

COOK INLET

- - - - Northern Route
- - - - Southern Route (the 1985 route)

At first light I headed out of Unalakleet before anyone else. My dogs seemed happy to reach the coast; maybe they could tell they were closer to home. I had to leave Stripe behind, because his feet were a little sore. The checkers would take care of him and ship him by plane to Nome.

As we climbed the hills on the way to Shaktoolik, a storm was picking up. By the time we hit the flats, it was blowing snow in our faces, and I stopped to put on warmer clothes. A

Lightly blowing snow on the way to Unalakleet turned into a blizzard by Shaktoolik.

big crowd turned out in the bad weather to welcome me. I knew a lot of the people in the village, and had worked there for a while when I first moved north. They were excited that I was in front!

The storm had turned into a blizzard, and I had some hard decisions to make in the hours ahead. I knew how dangerous these storms could be, but I didn't want the other mushers to catch me when I'd worked so hard to get ahead. If they did, everyone would wait until the weather got better, and then sprint on to Nome—and the faster teams would get me.

But was it worth risking my life for? I was scared, but I had worked too hard, for too many years, to let a blizzard stop me. I fed the dogs, and while they rested, I ate with friends. From inside, the weather looked even worse.

I called Joe in Nome from the one phone in town, and he told me to get out there, get going. But I knew he would say that even if there was a tornado, and it was 200 below. I was the one who had to decide. In a daze, I watched myself, not quite believing it, as my own feet took me around in the snow, getting ready to head out into the storm. I collected my dry gear and booted up all fifty-six paws. Another musher pulled in, and when he saw me getting ready to head out, he shook his head in disbelief. This made me feel a little stubborn and helped to get my feet moving.

The dogs seemed to think that if I was willing to go, so were they. I never doubted that they could make it. If anyone was the weak link in this chain, it was me. I pulled the hook. "Okay gang. Let's go." They shook the snow off and we started out of the village.

"This is *crazy*!" I kept saying to myself over and over as we drove into the swirling snow. It was like a war in my head. I could hardly see anything; everything was white and moving. "This is a *race*!" I argued. I was going to do what I promised myself in the beginning: the best I could.

As the sun dipped into the Bering Sea, the temperature dipped with it. Fifty, maybe sixty below with the wind chill. Fear made me careful. I felt like a hunted animal; there was no relief from the relentless weather. I couldn't see from one marker to the next, so we'd travel as far as we could from the marker behind us without losing sight of it, then I'd hook down the team and walk ahead, fighting the gusting north wind, until I found the next marker. Then I'd go back for the dogs. Inch by inch we crawled across the sea ice. The visibility was about what it would be like if you were wading through a box of baby powder, except this white stuff had sharp, cutting edges.

31

Out on the sea ice, losing the markers could mean stumbling through bad ice and ending up with a quick trip to the Happy Hunting Grounds. No, I wasn't ready to die yet.

The dogs sensed the intensity of the situation. Despite the wind that screamed in their ears and the ice that froze on their fur, they were game as long as I was. We trusted each other. They could have turned around and bolted back to Shaktoolik while I looked for markers up ahead, but they didn't. They curled up as only northern animals can, and patiently waited for me.

It was slow going, but death in the form of open water and hypothermia lurked on either side of the trail, so I stayed focused. One marker, then another. I was already pushing my luck. My clothes were getting wet from the inside out as I battled for every step. I'd learned the hard way on several other trips how miserable it felt to start getting chilled in damp clothes, how easily the heat seeped out. For now I was warm and running on pure adrenaline. Fortunately, I still had a few pieces of dry clothing in the sled. Whether I could get into them without freezing my hands was still to be seen.

One thing was certain. I wasn't turning back. Each step was too hard won. I tackled the blizzard like some summit-crazed mountaineer.

As daylight faded, it became even harder to see. The risk of getting lost grew worse. I realized that I wasn't going to be so lucky as to have the lights of Koyuk guide me across to the checkpoint. There would have to be a break in the battle. I was shutting down for the night.

$\mathcal{J}$ stopped the sled next to a trail marker and fought for a while with the frozen sled bag zipper. A raven sped by on the wind above us, the only other creature crazy enough to be out in this weather. I found the bag of snacks and gave each dog several pieces. By the time I'd emptied the sled, they were curled in the snow, in weather-proof circles.

Villagers in Shaktoolik watched as I prepared to mush out into the storm.

The sled bag was small, but big enough for me to crawl into and get away from the wind. It was such a relief. For a moment I lay on my back and the darkness spun like black snow. There I was, in a deadly arctic blizzard, protected by a thin nylon skin, warmed by the knowledge that I'd survived.

Then I started to get cold.

The fun wasn't over yet. I knew I'd have to change into my dry clothes somehow without freezing my fingers. If I stayed in the wet clothes, hypothermia would find me. There was no choice.

The sled bag was much smaller than a tent, so changing clothes inside it was out of the question. I had to unzip the bag, perform one step of my clothing routine, then scoot back into shelter to thaw out my hands before performing the next step. It took a couple of hours to change into dry clothes and get situated into my sleeping bag, but it was mighty cozy when I finally did. I slept mindlessly, switching from side to side on the hard basket slats.

Pile jacket

Medium-weight jacket

Eskimo-style pullover parka

Eskimo-style mukluks

Felt boot liners

Thermal socks

Insulated snow bibs

Wool leggings

Insulated gloves

Fur mittens

Mitten liners

Goggles

Turtleneck shirt

Wool sweater

Neck warmer

Musher hat

Plastic (not metal!) sunglasses

When I woke up on the 16th day of the race, it was getting light. I was shamelessly warm in my bag and had no intentions of going anywhere soon. I drifted back into oblivion. Then I woke up again, suddenly realizing that if I didn't get up and get going, I might have to spend *another* night out on the ice. I had no dry clothes for back-up and now my sleeping bag was probably damp as well.

I searched around inside the bag for the gloves I'd stashed for drying. Then I got my arms out so I could reach the zipper of the sled bag. For a panicky moment, the zipper refused to budge, frozen shut. Then I ripped it open. The cold bit into me as I peeked out.

I noticed I was talking to myself, walking myself through each step, keeping myself calm.

"Okay, where are the gloves? Put on the gloves."

"That's good. Now the first thing you do when you're up is hop into your mukluks."

"Do you have them ready? Good. Okay, open the zipper and go!" I managed to slip into the mukluks without the wind knocking me down.

The storm wasn't close to blowing itself out yet. It was as bad or worse than the day before. I couldn't see the next marker, but there was still one right there next to the sled, waiting patiently like an old friend.

The dogs were so buried, I wasn't sure which lumps were them. I called them up. "Hey huskies! Up we go!"

Feeding the team at Ophir earlier in the race, when bad weather shut things down for a day and a half. It was snowing, but at least we could see.

They popped out of their snowy beds like grouse. They yawned and stretched. I went to each dog, petting the ice off. I gave each one a snack of lamb. Their double coat of fur had kept the cold out. They were rested and ready to go. I wasn't hungry, but I made myself eat some Norwegian chocolate and chase it with Eskimo power food: seal oil. Then we hit the trail.

Once we were moving, it was a real struggle to keep from freezing my face. The Native-style fur ruff on my parka provided some protection, but I had to go without goggles because I couldn't see the markers with them on. My eyes grew raw as I wiped first one, then the other, with my mittened hand, straining to see the markers.

Back at Shaktoolik, the other mushers were more worried about me being hurt than having me beat them. They sat inside until late morning, drinking coffee and eating hotcakes and hoping the weather would get better. But it didn't. Outside the storm hammered the walls and wailed through the stovepipes. Snow pelted the windows and doors looking for any crack. No one wanted to go out, but it was still a race. A few of them finally headed out into the wind around 11 a.m. By then, I had been on the trail for a couple of hours. My friends around the state worried, hoping I was safe and could pull it off.

In Nome, Joe told them to wait before they sent out search and rescue, that I could handle it, that I wouldn't turn back.

Traveling in the storm was still incredibly difficult. If my dogs and I ever did get across to the other side of the ocean ice, I was going to kiss the snow bank. In an effort to keep my parka dry, I'd pulled my rain poncho on, belting it down with a rubber bungee cord. Then I stuffed polar fleece dog booties next to my face to keep it from freezing. Another handful of booties filled the gaps in the hood that the wind tried to find.

ime went by slowly. Dugan put his nose down and muscled straight into the wind. He remembered the trail from last year and knew Nome was out there somewhere. I put other dogs in lead, trying to give him a rest. Dusty led reluctantly, with his tug line slack, but it was worth it for a while because he seemed to have a knack for following the markers. But I ended up having to put Dugan back in before long. It would have been tough going without him. We were making pretty good progress when all of a sudden, there were no more markers and the ice looked new and green and dangerous.

Quick! What to do? Maybe Sister will know. I switched her to lead and hoped for the best. Halfway across the bad ice, I started to think Sister was taking us too far off course, and I yelled over the wind at her, "Gee! Sister, gee!" trying to get her to go to the right. But Sister had her own plan and kept stubbornly pulling us off to the left. The sled couldn't have stopped on the slick ice anyhow, so I held on and let them go. Then, like a mirage, a trail marker appeared! Sister had found the trail! We were back on the safe ice and I hooked down and ran up to give Sister a big fat hug and a kiss on her scarred face. "Good Girl! You're SOOOOO smart! Good job!"

The village of Koyuk was just ahead. Never had any sight looked sweeter. Snowmachines were already on their way out to meet us. "We did it! We really did it!" I said to the dogs. My friend Vira came and gave me a big hug.

Everyone was asking me questions, but mostly I just wanted to get my dogs bedded down and fed. I gave them beds of straw, a warm meal, and each one a thorough going over. Luckily, because the village is on a south-facing hill, we were a bit protected from the storm.

Inside Vira's house, I couldn't believe how good it felt to be out of the wind. My ears still hummed with the roar of it and my face was hot and wind-burned. I covered the house with wet clothes, hanging them wherever there was room. A few hours later, after a short sleep and the little I could eat of the huge turkey dinner Vira had made, I looked out the window across the ice and still couldn't see the headlights of any mushers following me. I hoped they hadn't gotten lost. It was still storming, but it was time for me to go.

The wind wasn't quite as bad as it had been. My team and I traveled cross-wise to it now, west towards Elim. There I had hotcakes with bacon grease on top at my friends', Fritz and Bessie's. I decided I would have to leave Sister in Elim. It was so hard to leave behind a member of the team, but Sister had a little bit of frostbite on her belly, so it would be safer to leave her with the checker. "We'll see you in Nome, Sweetie," I said, scratching her neck. "Thanks for all the help."

p "Little McKinley," down to Golovin, over to White Mountain. I was so tired it was all a blur. At the next checkpoint, I fed my dogs as they rested in the afternoon sun. A veterinarian checked the dogs and told me what I already knew: they looked great. Joe and some friends surprised me by showing up. I was glad to see them, but it seemed weird. I was still racing and not ready to relax. A short nap just made me sleepier, but my dogs and I drove down the river and were soon in the Topkok Hills. Once we were out of the hills onto

Some years in the Topkok Hills, traveling is easy; other years, the wind can almost blow you into the sea.

the lagoon, the wind picked up again. Several times I got blown right over, with the dogs dragging me through the snow until I could get them to stop. They would look back at me, impatiently wondering what the delay was. They seemed to have picked up speed, as though they knew we were getting close to the end.

Somehow in the dark, we took a wrong trail. It was two in the morning, but a light was on in one of the few cabins. I knocked on the door. "Where am I?" I asked the old Native man who answered. His eyes twinkled when he saw who stood on his porch. "Don't worry," he said. "Those guys won't catch you! You're in Solomon. Just go right over there, and it will take you to the Safety checkpoint."

The team resting at Safety before the final stretch into Nome.

So, turning around, with my headlight batteries almost gone, I started out again. After a few miles, I noticed something funny. I was looking at sled dog tracks. I was the only team out there, so it didn't take too long to figure out I had gotten turned around and was following my own trail and going back the way we had come! It's so easy to make mistakes when a person is tired.

It seemed like it took forever to get to the Safety checkpoint. I knew the other mushers were several hours behind me, so I had some soup and lay down for a while before heading out on the final stretch to Nome.

The sun was just coming up over the Bering Sea when we left the checkpoint. The dogs were pulling strong, Axle and Dugan leading the team. The Arctic is so beautiful and this was the best way to see it. I was sad that soon it would be over. I switched on my radio just in time to catch Hobo Jim's Iditarod Trail song. He was singing, "There are no sled tracks in front of me and no one on my tail. I did, I did, I did the Iditarod Trail."

It felt like the song had been written just for me, for that exact place and time. The tears froze on my face as I finally let myself believe that we were actually going to win this race. Not even a tidal wave or an earthquake could knock us out of first place now.

Closer to Nome, people started coming out on snowmachines, taking pictures, waving and smiling. I waved back. The dogs were excited too, and I started to run. I was so proud of them, I thought my heart would burst.

There was the finish line, and hundreds and hundreds of people, all cheering for us. I had done my best, and even surprised myself.

Sister was watching the race on TV at the checker's house in Elim as they interviewed me at the finish line. The announcer asked me what it felt like to win. Without thinking, I said, "What it feels like, is if I die now, it'll be okay."

Of course I didn't die then, and I'm still having adventures with my dogs, living a life I dreamed up when I was a kid.

It took a while to sink in that I had really won the Iditarod. All over the world, newspapers published the picture of me with Dugan and Axle at the finish line—the first woman ever to win the Iditarod Sled Dog Race! I was so proud of those dogs! And my mom and dad were so proud of me! They flew up to join me at the awards banquet.

Yellow roses for my leaders, Dugan and Axle, at the finish line.

The last few steps of the thousand-mile race!

nd there were more awards to come. I'm not sure which was the most exciting—getting a telegram from President Reagan, having Dugan and Sister get the Golden Harness Award for being the best leaders that year, or winning the Humanitarian Award for the best treatment of dogs on the race. I was honored in New York City by the Women's Sports Foundations as their pick for Professional Sportswoman of the Year, which made me quite proud for our whole sport. Then I was invited to Las Vegas to receive a Victor Award for Excellence in Sports, along with a handful of the country's finest athletes, all of whom I felt most honored to meet.

I was glad that lots of people who had never heard about dog mushing now knew more about it. I think that's part of why I started sharing my Iditarod experiences by writing books and visiting schools. It was especially fun writing about my cat, Danger, and all of his husky friends.

All the dogs on the team went on to live long and resourceful sled dog lives, although Axle had to retire when he was just seven because of arthritis. That's when his new career as my

Sister and Dugan recognized at the awards ceremony in Nome.

Iditarod champion Martin Buser and I representing Alaska at the inauguration of President Bill Clinton.

sidekick started. I took him everywhere with me, reasoning that if he couldn't run in the team, he still needed a way to get out and about. He rode everywhere in the truck with me, went to schools all over, and even joined me in President Clinton's Inaugural Parade. I even took him to Europe when I raced over there, mostly because I would have missed him too much if I had left him at home. Dugan finally retired when he was fourteen, and even then, he didn't want to quit. Most of the best lead dogs I've had since have been Dugan's sons and daughters.

Dugan was the father of many leaders, like Polar, Noodle, Buffy, Xerox, Ace, Pesky, and Picard.

Playing with Beastie's pups, Beamer, Belinda, and Bungee.

I feel so lucky to have been able to have this kind of life and all these great adventures. I've traveled to faraway places, met all kinds of

Dugan, Axle, and Bugs in retirement in Wasilla, with McDange, my new cat.

great people, and most of it has been because of these wonderful animals I get to live with. People ask me if it isn't a lot of work to have so many dogs. I smile and say, of course it is, but it's worth it! I wonder where we'll go next . . .

To my Mom and Dad. Thanks for always believing in me. —L.R.

To my faithful white shadow, Cirrus. —S.C.

Libby Riddles lives in Homer, Alaska. She has published three books and gives inspirational lectures about her experiences. The rest of the time she's out running her forty dogs!

Shannon Cartwright has been illustrating the best-selling PAWS IV children's books for more than twenty years. She and her husband live in the Talkeetna Mountains, near Denali.

Iditarod® is a registered trademark of Iditarod Trail Committee, Inc.

Published by Sasquatch Books
Manufactured in China in August 2012 by C&C Offset Printing Co. Ltd. Shenzhen, Guangdong Province

12   15 14

Book design: Kate Basart
Illustrations: Shannon Cartwright
Photographs: All photographs copyright by Libby Riddles, with the exceptions of the following: pages 19 and 33, copyright Jim Brown; page 45, top, copyright Jeff Schultz/Alaskastock.

Library of Congress Cataloging in Publication Data
Riddles, Libby.
        Storm Run / by Libby Riddles ; illustrations by Shannon Cartwright.
        p. cm.
        Originally published: 1st ed. Homer, AK : Paws IV Pub., 1996.
ISBN 1-57061-298-6 (hrdcvr) — ISBN 1-57061-293-5 (pbk. : alk paper)
Riddles, Libby—Juvenile literature. 2. Iditarod Trail Sled Dog Race, Alaska—Juvenile literature. 3. Mushers—Alaska—Biography—Juvenile literature. 4. Women mushers—Alaska—Biography—Juvenile literature. [1. Riddles, Libby. 2. Mushers. 3. Women—Biography. 4. Iditarod Trail Sled Dog Race, Alaska. 5. Sled dog racing.] I. Cartwright, Shannon, ill. II. Title.
SF440.15 .R54 2001
798.8'3'092—dc21
[B]   2001020966

SASQUATCH BOOKS /1904 Third Avenue, Suite 710 / Seattle, WA 98101/ (206)467-4300
www.SasquatchBooks.com / custserv@SasquatchBooks.com

Dugan